LANDSLIDE

A STORY OF FAITH, HOPE, AND LOVE.

TERRIE GARDNER

Dedication

This book is dedicated to my four children: Erika, Jerad, Rachael, and Daniel. There were struggles in my life that I have never shared with you, or anyone for that matter. I have held them close to the vest for too long. When I first began writing, it was a way to release the feelings that I had bottled up over the years. After several drafts, I realized I had released those feelings and I was free. That freedom allowed me to create what I hope to be an encouragement to you and others who read it. Just know that no matter how difficult the road, there is light to guide the way and you are never alone.

The decisions I made were not always right, and not always easy. I made many mistakes along the way. Love for my family and faith in God gave me the strength to keep going. You have supported and encouraged me to tell my story. With you all, I am stronger. I love you with every fiber of my being.

Mom

1 Corinthians 13:13

*And now these three remain: faith, hope, and love-
and the greatest of these is love.*

The Apostle Paul

CONTENTS

INTRODUCTION:

While attending a writing class at our local library, the instructor told us to ask ourselves this question, "Should your story be told? If so, why?"

My answer was, "Yes."

I want those who read my story to know that no matter what you are going through, you are not alone. This is my testimony of faith, hope, and love.

PROLOGUE

My cell phone rang just as I walked into the meeting, the voice on the other end was young and scared; it was my youngest daughter. "Mom, something's wrong with Daddy. He is laying on the floor, and I don't think he's breathing."

The feeling that came over me was just as I expected it would be, as if the world stopped just long enough for my heart to stop beating. I took a breath, and as that breath came, so did the words, "Do you feel a heartbeat? See if there is a heartbeat. Put your hand on his chest or feel for a pulse. Just see if you can feel his heart beating." I heard the phone as it hit the nightstand, and then there was silence for a few minutes. It seemed like forever until I heard her voice again. Was I prepared to hear what she would say?

CHAPTER 1

In 1985, my parents welcomed me and my two children into their Amarillo home, the one I grew up in. My life in Dallas hadn't worked out, so I was glad to be home. Dallas had been too big and too difficult. I told my parents the living arrangements would only be temporary until I could get on my feet.

I found employment quickly at a trade school as a recruiter. My job was to enroll students into the different programs the school offered. After the paperwork was done and before they started class, I would take them around to see the campus.

One day, while giving a tour, a prospective automotive student and I walked into the shop where the sound of racing engines and the smell of oil and gas filled the air. The cars were lined up with opened hoods, and students were bent over the fenders with tools in hand. I looked around for the instructor, so that I could introduce the student and myself since I had not met him yet. There was a small group of young people that were dressed in solid blue uniforms, and, in the middle of them, stood a man wearing black dress pants, a white shirt, a black tie, a blue lab coat, and sunglasses. His hair was dark brown and came just to the collar of the crisp white shirt that seemed so out of place. As we approached, he moved toward us and reached out to shake our hands.

"Hi, I'm Douglas Durham, Director of Automotive," he said as he removed his dark sunglasses revealing the most beautiful blue eyes I had ever seen. I remember thinking how handsome he was, and, as he turned toward the light, I saw the slightest sparkle in his eyes just before he put the sunglasses back on.

I smiled and said, "Hi, my name is Terrie. I am the new class recruiter, and this is your new student."

After the introductions were over, we said goodbye and turned to walk away. After a few steps I turned slightly to look behind me and get another look. To my surprise he had done the same.

The Automotive Program was popular, and I was taking quite a few students on tour almost daily. Doug was always welcoming and never seemed to be bothered by the disruption. He always made sure to introduce himself and take the time to walk the new student around and explain the program. It wasn't long before we became friends and had lunch together in the break room a few days a week. Our lunch of choice was Dr Pepper, crunchy Cheetos, and peanut M & M's. I was very impressed at how smart he was, and how he enjoyed learning and studying about the automotive industry, the new wave of technology, and where it was headed in the future. He always had an automotive manual or technology magazine with him as we sat eating our lunch, but always made time to talk and ask about my day.

"Reading and learning are important," he would say. "Things are moving fast; I have to keep up with it."

We got to know each other over time. I told him about my two kids, and that I was a single mom who had just moved back to Amarillo from Dallas. We talked about my growing up in Amarillo and graduating from Amarillo High School. He shared that he was married but separated. He was trying to make it work, but it was difficult. He didn't go much deeper than that. He was soft spoken with a very dry sense of humor. He had a slight grin and rarely smiled, but when he did, it was great.

On the 4th of July 1985, the school was going to be part of a parade in a small town outside of Amarillo. It was an annual event to promote the school and encourage new enrollment. The school had a trailer that the students would decorate and turn into a parade float. Everyone would pile on, wave signs about the school, and throw candy to the crowd. All employees were encouraged to attend and ride on the float, so I planned to go, and Doug offered me a ride.

He drove a black, two-door Mercury Capri with red pinstripes, a red interior with bucket seats, and an eight-track player. His music of choice was Pink Floyd, Meatloaf, or Journey. When I laughed and asked him where the country music was, he smiled and responded, "This car doesn't play country."

The drive gave us a chance to talk a little more in depth, and I learned a lot about him that day. He was born and raised in Levelland, Texas, a small town just outside of Lubbock. He had one sister who was married with three girls, a mom who lived in Levelland, and his dad had passed away. Doug graduated from Levelland High School (home of the Lobo's) and attended South Plains College—a small-town boy with big ideas. He told me that he had gotten really sick several years prior with spinal meningitis and wasn't expected to live. He suffered for quite some time unable to leave the house, and, as a result, was left with extreme sensitivity to light and severe migraines. That was the reason, he explained, that he wore sunglasses day and night; light could trigger a migraine that would sideline him for a couple of days. He was prescribed a migraine medication and a pain medication to manage them.

At one point, he reached into the collar of his shirt and pulled out a necklace. Hanging from it was a Saint Christopher, the saint of protection. He said it was given to him by a friend when he had been so ill. He told me that he never took it off.

At the age of nineteen, he had opened his own automotive shop and had built a good business. He was doing quite well with the shop, had met a girl, fell in love, and got married. After a few months, she decided Levelland wasn't the place for her and wanted to live in Amarillo, so he closed the shop, moved, and took a teaching job at the school.

We talked about what we liked to do for fun, and he told me he really liked to go to the Drags. Drag racing was his sport of choice. I had only been to the races a few times in my life and didn't know the difference between drag racing or any other kind of racing. He explained in terms I would understand, that drag racing was two cars, side by side, going down a straight track at a high burst of speed. He told me that not only did he like to go to the drag races, but that he owned a dragster, had formed his own racing team, and had raced all over the country. He told me that his dragster was parked at the school in a trailer, and that he would show it to me sometime. His exact words were, "It's trick."

When he talked about racing, the energy in his voice changed, and it was obvious how much he loved it. His spirit would light up.

Racing started in his early years, first on bicycles followed by high performance motorcycles. He told me a story about a hot, dusty West Texas day, when, after having worked for hours on a motorcycle, it was finally ready for a test run. He took the motorcycle across the street to a cleared cotton field to open it up as he had done so many times in the past. He drove it up and down the unpaved road, dirt flying behind him and circling the air as he shifted through each gear listening to every sound and feeling every movement it made. He had ridden bicycles and motorcycles in that field all his life, and that test run was just business as usual. As he tore across the field, he was satisfied that he had made all the repairs and adjustments needed. Just as he turned for home, the bike hit a drainage pipe in the bar ditch which caused it to go end over end. He went sailing one way and the bike another, both traveling several feet before hitting the ground. It took several minutes before he could focus and realize he was injured. His shoulder was hurt, and he didn't have to see it to know how bad it was. As he stood up, he realized he couldn't move his left arm. He reached up with the other hand and felt a bone protruding from his shoulder. There was no one around to call out for help, so he had to walk home, but first he had to check the bike. He managed to pick the bike up off the ground and push it home.

"It took a few surgeries," he said, but his shoulder and collar bone had been repaired and held together with screws. He pulled his shirt down off his shoulder to show me the scar that was left. It still gave him trouble at times depending on what he was doing, but he had been given a prescription to help with the pain if he needed it.

It was a hot and sticky summer day, and, as he drove, I would glance over and notice just how handsome he was. His olive skin looked as though he had a tan that never seemed to fade, and his chestnut brown hair lay perfectly. His nails were trimmed and clean, but his hands were callused and looked strong as he gripped the steering wheel and changed gears. He just didn't fit the stereotypical "grease monkey" type. Even in this heat he wore a long sleeve, button down shirt with the sleeves rolled up. He always looked nice. He wanted to set an example to those in his field and those he taught. He never referred to himself or his students as mechanics—they were automotive technicians. He was adamant about teaching and portraying an automotive technician as a professional, not the stereotypical grease monkey. He presented himself and his trade to his students and others as a profession to be proud of. He was good at his job and had the respect of his counterparts and automotive technicians around the state of Texas. His name was synonymous with great work.

Our friendship grew after that day; we shared more life stories—some good some bad. He met my two kids, Erika and Jerad, and they formed an immediate bond after he took them out to ride a small three-wheeler he had gotten for his nieces. He and some of the students helped me move out of my parents' house into an apartment. We drove up to the school to pick up the trailer, and I will never forget the look on the faces of my kids when he opened the doors that exposed a beautiful red and black dragster. Doug spent quite a bit of time hanging out with us on weekends. His marriage had fallen apart, and there was no hope of fixing it. He told me that his wife was pregnant, and he had tried so hard to make the marriage work, but it wasn't going to. His wife had filed for divorce. Even though the marriage didn't work out, he was looking forward to becoming a daddy.

We supported each other in our struggles, and, eventually, that friendship grew into what would become a great and wonderful love. We were married in Amarillo at my parents' house. It was a small, simple wedding, but those we loved most in the world were there, including my two children, Erika and Jerad, and his little girl, Rachael. We didn't have the time or the money for a honeymoon, so we booked a one-night stay at a local hotel and my parents watched the kids.

It was only a few hours later that evening when the phone rang. It was my mom, she said, "I hate to bother you, but Erika is running a pretty high fever and she is crying for you. She is pretty sick, what do you want me to do?"

I looked at Doug, shook my head, and he got up to pack our bag.

I said, "It's okay, Mom, tell her we are on our way."

CHAPTER 2

Eventually we moved to Doug's hometown of Levelland, population 13,000. We rented a small place close to the elementary school and a Baptist church. Small town life was exactly as I had expected—everyone knew your name. It felt good, it felt safe, and it would be a good place to raise a family.

Doug had found a job teaching at a large technical school in Lubbock with a commute of about an hour a day. The drive took a toll on him, and his migraines became worse. The doctors had given him a couple of new drugs that were supposed to control the headaches a bit better, but nothing was keeping them under control. He didn't complain, but it was obvious he was struggling. He spent many hours alone in our bedroom in the dark with a cool cloth on his head, waiting out the pain.

We wanted to buy our first home, and we found a perfect one that sat on almost two acres. Unfortunately, the down payment was more than we had saved, and we thought we would have to pass it up. To my surprise, he decided that the time had come to stop thinking of racing and start thinking about the family, so he sold the dragster and the trailer for the down payment. The day that trailer rolled out of the yard attached to someone else's truck was a very hard day indeed. To this day my children blame me, in jest, for Doug selling it and never racing again. We bought our house, made a home, and it wasn't long before I would discover that I was pregnant.

It was early September, and I had just had my twenty-eighth birthday. It was a Monday afternoon and the state fair had just opened in Lubbock about thirty miles away. The trade school where Doug worked had a booth at one of the fair exhibits. Doug was supposed to be there to recruit students, so I went along to help. We took Erika and Jerad to his mother's house and would pick them up later that night.

It had been raining off and on all day. By the time we left for home, it was pouring, and the drive was difficult. There were cars pulled off to the side of the road all along the way. The rain was coming down so hard you could barely see the road in front of you. The windshield wipers were going as fast as they could, but they could not keep up with the amount of water pouring from the dark gray sky. The storm was powerful with lightning, and the booming thunder so hard it would vibrate the truck. All around us were tornado sightings. The drive took longer than usual, but we made it back and headed to pick up the kids. After bundling them into jackets and blankets, we battled our way back to the car against strong wind and rain. As we neared the street that lead to our house, we saw flashing lights and roadblocks. We pulled over to find out what was going on, and the officer said the street was flooded and closed at both ends.

We wouldn't be able to get home that night, so we turned the car around and went back to his mom's house to wait out the storm. When we arrived, she told us that she had gotten several calls asking if we were okay because our street was under water. We put the kids to bed, and Doug decided he would not be able to sleep until he checked our house. He went into his old bedroom, put on some old waders, unlocked the gun safe, and reached for his gun. He told me he would be back shortly and would find our two cats and bring them back with him. As he bent to kiss me good-bye, I stood up, grabbed some trash bags and walked to the door. He tried to tell me not to go, but I was already out the back door and in the truck.

While we were driving, he asked me what I was going to do with the trash bags. I said I was going to tape them on my legs to keep my feet and pants dry. He got a chuckle out of that, and so did I. As we drove back toward our house, we could see the entire area was covered in water. The road looked like a river and was rushing into lawns and driveways. We slowly made our way to the end of our street. We couldn't drive any closer since the water was too deep, so we pulled over and parked the truck. I stepped into the garbage bags, and Doug taped them as tight as he could to my legs to keep the water out. We started walking, and, as we walked, the water got deeper, colder, and darker. I was six months pregnant and took every step as carefully as possible. Doug tried to get

11

me to go back to the truck, but I was determined to see what, if anything, had been damaged at home and to find the cats. We made our way through the thigh-high water to the front door of our house.

I said, "I'm afraid to open the door. All the water is going to get in the house." Doug pulled out the key, unlocked and opened the door, and, as we stood there, water came rushing out of the house. The water was about three and a half feet deep throughout the house. As we shined the flashlights around, we could see our furniture floating, and I began to cry. (All I could think of was, not again. I had lost everything I owned in a fire while living in Dallas a few years earlier.) I walked slowly and could feel the carpet coming up from the floor. I couldn't believe it; how could this happen and where were my cats? We walked from room to room calling them, and, as we walked through the kitchen to the hallway that led to the back bedrooms, I noticed a glow under the water from the night lights plugged into the wall. It was dark and quiet, and the eerie sight of the night lights gave way to fear. Due to the shock of that night, we hadn't thought about the power being on until that moment. The smell of gasoline filled the air and grew strong as we got closer to the garage. We had a motorcycle and a three-wheeler that were floating upside down and the fuel was running through the house. In the quiet, I heard a faint cry and found one of our cats in the windowsill of my son Jerad's room unable to move. I stepped over toy cars, little boy shoes, and the mattress from the bed until I was able to reach the window and hold one terrified cat in my arms.

We found the other floating on a board in the garage. Grabbing him wasn't going to be easy because the ground was slick, and our footing was unsure. Doug told me to make my way back to the front door and get out of the house. He would get the cat and meet me there. As I headed back to the front door, I heard a thump and a moan soon followed by Doug carrying the cat, both soaking wet. He assured me he was fine, and we began our trek back to the truck.

We had only lived in the house three weeks when this happened. It took three months to get our house livable again, and we lived with his mom while the work was being done. We would talk about that night for years to come and how God's hand had been on us as we walked through the house. With the power on and all the electrical outlets being live, it was by God's grace that we were not electrocuted. We knew without a doubt that Doug, the cats, me, and our unborn baby were wrapped in His protective arms. We moved back into our house on Christmas Eve, and our son, Daniel, was born four days later. He was perfect.

Six weeks after Daniel was born, Doug received a letter from his ex-wife offering him custody of his daughter, Rachael. He was shocked, as was I because we had to fight for every visit he was given, and we worried daily about her well-being. There was no question that he wanted custody. The situation was difficult; his ex was unstable and had severe mood swings.

We loaded up the kids and drove two hours to Amarillo. Once there, we called an attorney, got the paperwork ready, and set a time for her to sign the custody papers. When the papers were signed and filed, Doug and I drove to the house where they were living. As we pulled in front of the house, there were boxes, toys, and furniture sitting in the driveway. We loaded everything in the back of the truck, and Doug secured the car seat. He walked to the door, reached for his daughter, and, with tears in his eyes, walked away. We were a family of six now with an infant and a toddler. It was wonderful and exhausting at the same time.

CHAPTER 3

A few months later in 1987, we decided to re-open the automotive shop that Doug had started years before, so Doug wouldn't have to make the commute to and from Lubbock every day. I would manage the office, and he would manage the shop. It was teamwork at its best. We found a building that we could grow into that was big enough for an office, two bays, and one employee. With the two older kids in school, and I not wanting to leave the youngest two at daycare, we brought them to work with us. I had a playpen, highchair, and toys set up next to my office. I often would joke that Daniel learned to walk on the shop floor, and how I was surprised he had skin left on the bottom of his feet after the nightly scrubbings he would get. Our kids spent a lot of time in the shop. Sometimes on Saturday we would bring Erika and Jerad down to help clean. My oldest son still talks about having to pick up red rags. It was indeed a family affair. It worked, and we were happy.

As anyone knows, blended families are not easy. We had several issues with Doug's ex-wife at first, and then she just disappeared. We spoke to our attorney about my adopting Rachael. After a year of no contact we went to court as a family, and I legally adopted Rachael as my own. We were a family—we never used the words yours, mine, or step. It was always *ours*.

Our approach to auto repair was to provide teachable moments both to our techs and the owners of the vehicle. No job was complete until it was fully explained how and why it was being done. Other shops in town would bring transmissions to Doug to rebuild; he could take one apart and put it back together in his sleep. It almost looked like a surgical procedure—out came the lab coat, the surgical gloves, and the perfectly spotless shiny tools laid out on a red rag in order of use. Detailed and innovative, he would create learning tools out of broken car parts by cutting them in half, so he could explain how it was supposed to work. It was repurposing before repurposing was cool. There were few automotive technicians like him; his reputation and work ethic were undeniable. We were doing very well for ourselves. Business was great, and I was even doing radio commercials for the shop. Doug would laugh every time one of them came on the radio. He would say, "Stop what you're doing and listen! She's on the radio again." Then he would smile and say, "I love you, Darlin."

He knew so much about so many things, and, at times, I was simply amazed at his knowledge. He taught me a lot about automotive repair along the way, and some things I still remember. I was always awed by him but never told him that he was the smartest man I had ever known.

Climbing around under the hoods of cars and having to be a contortionist under a dashboard began to wear on him. Along with the regular migraine headaches and the ongoing pain in that shoulder, he began to have numbness in his right hand and arm. It was making gripping tools very difficult. After several visits to our family doctor, he made an appointment for Doug to see a neurologist and get some answers.

It was now March of 1991 and, after having gone through several tests, he was sent to see a neurosurgeon. We found out that he had spinal stenosis and needed surgery on his neck to repair it. The surgery would allow the doctor to trim off or remove part of the vertebra to widen the spinal canal and give the nerves more room. The doctor said it needed to be done right away.

By this time our company had grown, and our business had increased tremendously. After getting coverage arranged at the shop, surgery was scheduled. The doctor explained that the incision would start just below the skull and extend to his shoulder blade, and the scar would be significant. Doug was not a vain man, but he joked with the doctor about not taking too much hair off in the back, that he was in control of who gave him haircuts. The surgeon laughed and said he would do the best he could.

The surgery was supposed to take about three to four hours, but instead took much longer as the damage was worse than expected. The vertebra had closed so tightly around the nerves that the repair was extensive. We later found out that if he had not had the surgery and had had another neck injury, the vertebra would have probably severed his spinal cord, and he most likely would have been paralyzed from the neck down.

I was waiting outside of recovery when they rolled him into the hallway. He was groggy but able to ask me two questions: "Where are my sunglasses?" and "Do I still have my hair?"

I laughed and assured him that his hair was intact and then reached into my purse for his sunglasses. The surgeon smiled and raised the hair up just a bit to show me that he had shaved only the underside so that when Doug combed his hair down the scar would not show.

After several days in the hospital, he was released. The incision was healing fine, and he was able to get up and walk around. He left with a neck brace, instructions on recovery, and a handful of prescriptions. We were told that there had been reports of chronic lower back pain after this surgery in some cases, but it wouldn't be right away if it happened at all. The report said that due to the lack of neck support from this surgery the remaining vertebra would try to compensate and could result in this lower back pain. Doug wouldn't be able to return to work for quite some time as he was taking pain medication and muscle relaxers along with the regular migraine medication he had taken for years. Little did I know that this would be the beginning of a very hard road.

Though we were the busiest shop in town, I was able to manage it alone for a while. Our primary clients were oilfield fleet vehicles. We had a reputation of getting the trucks in and out quickly, and very seldom did they return the trucks for the same problem. We had integrity, and our word was important to us.

Things were going okay with Doug being out, but the service experience was never quite as good. Doug was the reason customers came to Automotive Services, so I was on the phone getting instructions and advice daily from him as he recuperated. One day, I called home to ask a question, and he didn't answer. I wasn't concerned because I knew I would be going home for lunch soon, and I would just talk to him about it then. When I got home, he was not in his usual spot waiting for me to come in, so I went looking for him. I walked into our bedroom and found him asleep, so I shook him a little to let him know I was home.

He mumbled, and I asked if he was okay or if he needed anything. I could tell he was not himself and was having a hard time staying awake to talk to me. I asked him why he was so sleepy, and he managed to get a few words out, but I couldn't understand what he was saying. Finally, he was able to tell me in slurred speech that it was because of his medication. I didn't know what to do. Would he be okay, or should I call someone? I decided to call the hospital emergency room and tell them what was going on and find out if I should be concerned. The nurse at the ER was very calm and asked me a few questions beginning with, "Is he breathing?"

"Yes, he is breathing."

"Does he seem to be breathing normally or is he having trouble?"

"He is breathing normally," I said.

"When he tries to wake up, does he look at you and know who you are?"

"Yes," I said.

She told me that he may have had a reaction to the medication, and to watch him to be sure he didn't have trouble breathing or develop any new issues. She said he should be fine but advised that I call and let his doctor know what had happened in case he might want to change the medication.

I stayed home the rest of the day watching him. When he finally woke up and was able to stay awake, I told him what had happened and how scared I was. He didn't remember any of it. I told him what the nurse had said about the medication and that we needed to talk to his doctor. He wasn't very happy that I had called the ER. He said that he hadn't been sleeping very well at night because of his neck and taking the medication on top of being so tired had just put him out. Okay, that made sense, but I told him to call the doctor the next day and let him know. I had no reason to doubt he would follow through. Looking back, I don't believe he ever made that call.

Eventually Doug was able to go back to work but was limited to what he could do. His being there took a lot of pressure off me and put more on the guys to get their work done. No muscle relaxer medications were taken at work, but he did take the pain medication. He would really be in pain by the end of the day, and, as warned, his lower back began to hurt. I didn't know how he would be able to do everything he needed to do at the shop with the problems he was having physically. I know his pain medication was changed and increased several times before the doctor finally had the right potion to keep the pain under control.

One night he had trouble walking from the living room to the kitchen. Doug was very unsteady when he got up from the chair and as he walked. I saw him stumble and almost fall. I got up from the sofa and reached for him, but he said he was fine. His words were not clear, and his bright blue eyes were glassy— almost like looking through a dirty window on a sky-blue day. I knew that talking to him was useless, so I waited. He never wanted to talk about his medication or how it made him feel or how it made him behave. Whenever I brought up the subject, he would say, "I'm fine."

One afternoon while Erika and some of her friends and I were gathered in the kitchen we heard a loud noise from the living room. I ran to see what had happened and found Doug on the floor. He had stumbled and fell onto the glass coffee table. I was afraid to look; I was sure he had broken the glass and cut himself badly. I was relieved to see that he was not injured and helped him up, walked him to our bedroom, and put him on the bed to sleep it off.

This was the first time I was sure there was a problem. I was so confused by this; I had no experience and no idea what I was dealing with. Doug was taking the medications given to him by medical professionals. I wasn't a professional, and they knew what they were doing right? Was this normal? Was it just a side effect? Whatever it was, I didn't like it. Should I talk to the doctor? I just didn't know.

Several months passed, and the shop returned to normal. It seemed like Doug wasn't taking as much medication as he had been. He was better, and I was glad.

One day as Doug was making some adjustments to the car lift in the rear of the shop, a customer came into the shop to ask a question. As I was talking with her, I heard metal hit the ground. I looked up to see Doug coming toward us holding a red rag to his head. I immediately got him into my office and cleaned the blood from his scalp to see how badly he was injured. An eighty-pound metal piece from the lift had fallen about fifteen feet and hit him in the top of the head. His skull was split open and blood was streaming down his face. I put him in the car and took him to the emergency room. Several hours, x-rays, and stiches later, they released him. They told us how lucky he was because a blow like that could have killed him. It didn't, but he was feeling the results of it.

After a follow-up visit to the family doctor, Doug shared that since he had been hit in the head, his shoulders and neck were really hurting. It was decided that the impact from the metal had shoved his neck down into his shoulders and that was what was causing all this new pain. He was given a prescription for new pain meds. This scared me. I reminded the doctor that he was already taking pain meds and muscle relaxers from the residual pain from surgery. The doctor told Doug to stop taking those, and that this new drug, Vicodin, would be much better.

We lived in the middle of cattle, cotton, and pump jacks. We were good at what we did and went the extra mile to get and keep business coming. Business was good, until it wasn't. In the early nineties, the oil field was taking a hit. Companies were selling most of their fleet vehicles or closing operations altogether. The industry was failing and taking us with them. We had to lay off a few people and downsize as our economy was in trouble. We were used to being three deep in the bays with several vehicles waiting to get in, so this slowdown was going to be hard to come back from.

Our shop was always a top buyer from the tool trucks that came by weekly. One of them had been a friend for a long time and told us about a position that was opening to do training classes in the area. It would mean travelling and being away from home, but it was a way for Doug to get out from under the hoods of cars every day and bring in extra money. He would be a contract employee and set his own classes, so that he could still run the shop. This would allow him to teach again and give us the supplemental income that we really needed. Money was getting tight and we had employees to pay, a mortgage, and kids to raise.

CHAPTER 4

With this new job, Doug seemed like a different person. He was happier than I had seen him in a very long time, and he had the sparkle back in his eyes that I had missed so much. In a week or so he had taught his first class in Lubbock and would continue teaching two or three nights a week for several months. One afternoon he got a call and was told about a teaching job in Oklahoma. They had heard great things about his work and really wanted to meet with him. After the meeting, they offered him the job with a great salary and package. We sat down and talked about it for a while; I could see the energy swell up inside of him and the pride of being considered the best in the business. I smiled and told him to go. I would run the shop, and everything would be okay. The following weekend he left for Oklahoma City.

One weekend a big storm blew through Levelland, leaving behind damaged cars, homes, and businesses. The shop was hit hard; the storm took the roof off in places and exposed tools, equipment, and records to the downpour of rain. We had so much damage we could hardly count it all. What the insurance didn't or wouldn't cover, we claimed as a loss to the IRS. This sent a red flag for an audit, and, after a week of going through what records we could salvage, the IRS came back to tell us that they would not allow the loss we had claimed. We were given a due date to come up with the funds. We now owed the IRS a lot of money.

Doug's time away increased, and I did my best to run the shop and take care of the kids. We were doing okay until the economy took another tumble and oil production basically stopped. Along with keeping the doors open, paying employees, running the house, and now the pressure from the IRS, I was stressed to the max.

One day I got a call from the bank that our accounts had been frozen by the IRS. We had gotten behind, and no matter how hard I tried to stay afloat, I was sinking. I had gotten letters and had made calls trying to get extensions and understanding, but, apparently, they had an agenda and taking everything seemed to be the answer. I called Doug and he got home as soon as he could. We had a hard decision to make. We would have to downsize and sell off some equipment to pay the IRS, and so, we did. It looked as though our business wasn't going to make it, and I must admit, I was not sad about it. I could not bear to deal with the stress and responsibility of it all any longer. With the accounts frozen, checks were bouncing, and I couldn't do anything about it. Some people were understanding, others weren't.

One day, I was working when a car from the Sheriff's Department drove up. Being a small town, we knew the officers by name. One of them came inside and quietly said that he had a warrant for my arrest—insufficient funds. I don't remember exactly what happened, but I think my knees buckled, and I almost went to the floor. Doug was there that day, and he begged them to take him instead, but it was my signature on the checks, so it was me that had to go in. The officer slowly walked me to his car and opened the back door; tears were flowing down my face as I sat down in the back of that car. The look on the deputy's face was one of sorrow and regret; he did not want to do this anymore than I wanted him to. He told Doug to follow us and post bail right away, so I would not have to go to jail. I remember thinking: How ironic, I am going to jail for having no money, and he says all we must do is pay my bail.

I remember that car ride and praying to God to please help me through this. We had cash stashed at the house and would get a bondsman for the rest. I felt so humiliated and afraid. I had never in my life been in trouble, except kid stuff with my parents. This was something I could not imagine in my wildest dreams. When we arrived at the station, the deputy opened my door and led me to the door of the jail. I saw a solid brown, windowless door and a box with a buzzer and a speaker. The deputy rang the buzzer, and the door opened. We stepped into a 6 ft x 6 ft space with a partial glass wall and a sliding window that was locked. Next to that there was another door, and, after speaking with the person on the other side of the glass, the door was opened. We stepped into a large room with a few on-duty officers, some of which I recognized and some that recognized me. I could see the look of utter shock on their faces. Some I knew from church, others I knew from living in this small town for so long. The deputy asked me to sit down for just a minute, and he said someone would come to speak to me. As he turned to walk away, he leaned over and said, "Terrie, I am so sorry."

I looked up with tear-filled eyes and gave the best smile I could and said, "It's okay, you are only doing your job."

A very nice officer came over and explained what was going to happen. First, they were going to take my fingerprints, so we walked over to an area with ink pads and cardboard. He took my hand and dipped each finger into the ink before pressing them on the cardboard. Secondly, he explained that I would stand in front of a camera so that they could take my picture. I asked for a tissue and wiped my eyes as I walked over and stood in front of a wall that had a measuring stick of some sort hanging next to it. I stood still looking ahead and then to the side, and tears began to flow again. I will never forget what the officer said to me when we were done, "That's the prettiest mug shot I have ever taken."

He took me over to a chair, sat me down, and said, "You wait right here. Doug is on his way." As he looked over in the corner he said, "I am not putting you in that holding cell."

For this I was thankful. I can honestly say I am not sure I would have been able to stand it. I was already close to a breaking point. It was a very short time, but it seemed like hours before Doug arrived with a bondsman. I was given information about a court date and appearing before the judge and told to be sure I didn't miss it. Then I was released.

Doug drove me home. It was late in the afternoon and the kids were home, but I made my way past them and into our bedroom and closed the door. I went into our bathroom, closed that door as well and sat down on the floor, back against the wall and cried. I felt defeated and ashamed. How could this happen? How did we get here? I should have managed the money better; I should have done things differently. I looked for the answers within myself, but they weren't there. I was angry, sad, and confused.

Being a Christian, I knew God loved me, but it didn't seem like the Jesus I trusted was anywhere to be found. Why was God allowing so much into our lives, and what had we done to deserve it? We had a churchgoing, God-fearing family. We worked hard, volunteered, helped those less fortunate, raised our children to know right from wrong, and instilled good morals and values in each one. I was always about service, and I served on the mission field in Mexico every summer. We served our church and were so regular in attendance that everyone knew which pew was ours. I didn't know if I could take any more stress—I was exhausted. Why was this happening? Why? I looked up and cried, "Okay God, I'm weak. I need you. Where are you?"

I stood up to get aspirin for my pounding headache, and I took a hard look at the face staring back at me in the mirror. I thought, *Now what? What's next?* I heard my voice say, "This is your fault, what are you going to do now?"

All I could see were the struggles, day after day, year after year, why? Every time I thought things were going well, BAM, another disaster hit. I didn't know if I could take anymore. As I reached for aspirin, I noticed all the bottles of prescription drugs lined up in front of me. I took two of them off the shelf and sat back down on the floor. Tears were streaming down my face. As I sat there contemplating the unthinkable, I heard a knock on the bathroom door and a tiny voice that said, "Momma?"

I put the pills back into the bottle, wiped my face, and opened the door. There stood my son with his tennis shoes dangling from the strings. He asked if I could help him get the knots out so that he could go outside. I reached down for the shoes, wiped a smudge from his face, and knelt to hold him tightly in my arms. He wiggled away and said, "Hurry, it will be dark soon."

In that moment I heard another voice in my head that said, "You are not done."

As the court date neared, my attorney said if we came up with the entire amount of money owed on the checks, the judge would probably dismiss the charges. If not, he could send me to jail. I was terrified. We sold as much equipment as we could, used every penny we had coming in, and even borrowed some from a friend. Doug and I felt so bad about borrowing that money that one evening we loaded up the beautiful red and black Snap-on collector toolbox along with Doug's most expensive tools and took it to their home. We told them that we would pay them back, but to keep the toolbox until we did. I appeared before the judge and told him I had the funds to pay restitution and apologized for what happened. He accepted it and let me go.

The shop was gone. Doug was still teaching on a contractual basis, and I started working part time. We were struggling financially, and we couldn't recover. Doug was travelling a lot for work but seemed to be doing so much better with the medications. He seemed stronger, and I was glad. One day, he came home from a trip to Oklahoma and told me that Snap-on Tools had offered him a full-time job to "Train the Trainer" but it was in Arizona. ARIZONA! They had set up a trip for us to go out and look. I agreed, but there was no way I was going to live in Arizona.

It was March of 1998 when we left the kids with Doug's mom and boarded a plane headed west. It was nice to get out of Levelland for a while, we hadn't been anywhere for a very long time. We needed this time together without the kids, without the stress of the everyday struggles. Even if it was temporary. The weather was perfect, and we lapped it up as we drove around looking at all the cities and towns in the area outside of Phoenix. We told the company that we would have to go home and discuss it, and we did.

I wasn't very excited about moving: my kids were happy here, my mother in-law and my parents lived nearby, and I loved my church family and my mission group. My life was in Levelland. How could I leave? Things weren't going well financially, and Doug was really pushing to make the move to Arizona. I just didn't want to do it!

One afternoon as I was walking into the house, I found a notification on the door. It was bright orange, and written in dark print I saw the word, "EVICTION". I tore it off the door and read the small print informing us that we had to evacuate the premises in seven days. We were behind on the house payments; we had been foreclosed on. I blamed myself. Because of all the efforts to keep me out of jail, we were losing our home. This news was devastating. What were we going to do? Where were we going to live? The embarrassment, the shame, the feeling of total failure swept over me. I went into the house clutching that orange piece of paper and picked up the phone to call Doug. I tried to keep my emotions under control as I spoke, but the shock and disbelief had overtaken me. All I could say was, "I need you to come home."

We found a rental down the street, and, in a few days, we left the house that I loved. As we were leaving with the last load, I looked back at the house that help so many memories. I pictured my kids running in the yard, the horses that played in the field, and the Christmas mornings filled with laughter and joy. I saw the living Christmas trees that we planted every year when the holidays were over, and I wiped away the tears as we drove away.

Doug was still teaching his classes, but the pressure was on to decide about Arizona. Do we stay and try to make things work here or do we move and make a fresh start? I was torn. The thought of moving so far away from our families was almost unbearable. Erika was graduating high school and did not want to move. She had already told me that if we moved, she would be staying in Levelland. My mother had recently been diagnosed with breast cancer and was undergoing treatment. How could we move so far away? How could we stay?

Doug was excited about the possibilities of moving, and there was no doubt about what he wanted to do. After lengthy discussions and remembering the beautiful mountains and palm trees that we saw in Arizona, it seemed the best thing to do was go. God had a plan. He never closes a door without opening another. He knew that we had to hit bottom before He could move us, literally. If we hadn't closed the shop and lost our home, we would have never made the move to Arizona. The Bible verse in Romans played over and over in my head.

Romans 8:28 - And we know that in all things God works for the good of those who love him.

CHAPTER 5

Doug accepted the position in Phoenix and was going to have to go ahead of us right away. The three youngest kids and I would move when school was out in May. The company put Doug up in a hotel until he could make other arrangements. There was no way that we could pay our rent and pay for a house in Arizona at the same time.

I knew that Doug would have to find someplace soon after he got to Phoenix. When we were there and had driven around looking at all the surrounding areas of Phoenix, we had made the decision that if we really did move to Arizona we wanted to live in Gilbert, a small township in the East Valley. We liked it because there were cotton fields and horses and it felt like home. I decided to call some Southern Baptist Churches in Gilbert. I thought if I called a sister church and explained the situation and told them we were Southern Baptist from Texas that I might find someone that had an apartment or a house or something where Doug could stay.

The first call I made was to the First Baptist Church of Gilbert, I spoke with the church secretary— her name was Patty— and told her our story and that my husband just needed a room to rent for a short time. I assured her we were good people and she could call my pastor and talk to him to verify my story. She told me she didn't really know of anyone in the church that could help but that she would mention it and see what happened.

About a week later, Patty called back and said that there was a couple that had moved to Arizona from Texas that were members of the church. They told her to get Doug's phone number and they would call him to set up a meeting. They felt that since we were fellow Texans they should try and help. Doug drove out to Gilbert to meet them, and after visiting for a while they invited him to move into their spare bedroom for the next couple of months until the rest of us arrived and we moved into our own place. They would turn out to be our best friends Bruce and Vicki. When I look back on it now, I know it was a "God Thing."

We were really moving, and it was not going to be easy. I had a lot to do, and I was doing it alone. We had gotten the last of the shop equipment sold, the packing done, a daughter graduated, and the day came to say goodbye. Leaving my daughter in Texas was a horrible feeling, but she was old enough to make her own choices, and they were not the same as ours. Doug came back to Levelland to load the U-Haul and drive with us to Arizona. After the last bit was loaded, Jerad, our then 16-year-old, said that he wanted to take the old, black Capri with us. Doug had promised him that when he got his driver's license, they would work on it together and it would be Jerad's to drive. Time was running out, but Doug went to U-Haul and got a trailer big enough to hold the Capri and hooked it up to the back of the truck. Everything was ready and we were leaving Levelland, a place that held memories of great joy and great sorrow. As we pulled away and I saw my daughter Erika waving goodbye, my heart was breaking, and I cried for miles as we drove away. I was afraid and a little excited, and I prayed we had not made the wrong decision. I felt this was what we were supposed to do but didn't understand why, I just had to have faith that I was right.

We settled into a beautiful rental house and began a new life in Arizona in the summer of 1998. Doug was enjoying his job, and everything seemed to be going well for all of us. The kids started school in late summer and did much better with the change than I expected. I was working for Doug part time from home making the training schedules and calling to remind people of class, as well as taking the payments and doing the paperwork for the company. When the medical insurance kicked in, we were able to get set up at a local doctor's office, and Doug was able to get all of his medical records transferred to Arizona. He had been doing so well that I almost forgot about the medication issues back in Texas. Originally, he was going into the office every day, but as time went on, he began working from home more often. Unfortunately, working at home gave way to easier use of his medications.

He was still taking the migraine medication, pain medications (two of them) and a muscle relaxer. It was during this time while working together from home that I began to see that his problem was worse than I thought. He was spending more time sleeping and a lot less time working. As usual, whenever I brought it up or questioned it, he always had the same things to say: I took it on an empty stomach; I forgot that I took it a couple of hours ago and took another one; I just need to lay down. I never doubted that he was in pain. It just seemed he was not getting any relief, and I couldn't understand why the doctors weren't doing something different to help him. I accepted and trusted that they were doing all they could do. I didn't question the doctor's decisions directly but questioned Doug instead. This would be a mistake I made more than once.

We joined First Baptist Church of Gilbert—the same one I had called a few months prior looking for housing for Doug. It was small and warm and friendly, and we felt like we belonged there. Our family got involved in the different ministries offered and were serving where we could.

The church had purchased land to build a bigger worship center, and, in a few months, we would be leaving the little church on Gilbert Road to a beautiful new location. It was Christmas 1999, and we had completed the first phase of a new building project. We were all preparing for the Grand Opening which would be the Sunday before Christmas. Everyone was so excited to go to church that morning because we would be in the new building for the first time and expected a very full house. We arrived for the service and found a place to sit in the back of the church. Our oldest son was sitting with friends about three or four rows behind us. The anticipation of a full house was correct; it was standing room only.

We sang a couple of songs, and, just as we were about to sing another one, Doug began to sway on his feet. I tried to hold him, but then he just went down. He was lying in the aisle of the new church, though only those in the immediate area could see what happened. The singing continued as I began to cry. I asked for help as I knelt on the floor next to him. The people around us began to move in, and I could see the fear in the faces of my youngest children. In a matter of seconds, my oldest son literally flew across the seats in front of him to get to us. Doug was white and unresponsive. I cried out in prayer, "No, Lord, no! Please, Lord, please let him be okay."

A nurse standing close by came to his side, loosened his tie and shirt, checked for a heartbeat, and began CPR. Someone else had called 911. His breathing was very shallow, and he was still unresponsive. After several minutes, he began to open his eyes, but it was a blank stare with no expression. Though I pretended I didn't, I knew what had happened and so did my children. The paramedics came, and after getting him stable, they loaded him on to the stretcher. I remember hearing Pastor Larry say to the crowd, "Right now, everyone prays for Doug." The music played softly as they took him out of the sanctuary.

I asked him quietly, "How many pills did you take before church?" We had had this discussion that morning. I had told him not to take anything because I didn't want him to fall asleep during the service. He looked at me and softly said, "I didn't take them." Then they loaded him into the ambulance.

I climbed into the front cab with the driver and left my crying children standing on the curb with friends. As we drove to the emergency room, I answered questions about Doug's health, history of illness, and the medications he was taking— all the normal routine questions that are asked by medical professionals. I gave them the information they asked for but nothing more. Was I protecting Doug, myself, or both of us? I still don't know. But I didn't want people to think badly of him, and I didn't want them to look at our family differently. As I sat in the waiting room, I thought this might be the answer, maybe an eye opener for Doug. Maybe it would stop here. I prayed for that as I sat alone with tears flowing down my face. I begged God to do something, to help us, to help Doug! I trusted and believed that everything was going to be okay.

Our friends from church came and brought the kids. They stayed with us while we waited to hear from the doctor. The waiting room was full of people that cared about my family. They were so worried, and I felt like such a fake standing there pretending that I had no idea what happened and all the while knowing. I couldn't let on. I had to keep pretending, and it was killing me.

The faces on my children spoke volumes. They were worried, of course, as they always were when Doug had taken too much medication, but this was different. This time we had to take him to the hospital; this time he fell hard; this time he was unconscious; and this time it was not in our home. Had the secret been revealed? Were we now going to have to explain to people what had been going on? A friend offered to take our youngest son, Daniel, to their house as her son was his best friend. He wasn't sure that he wanted to go. He felt he needed to stay and be there for his dad, but I convinced him that his dad would be fine, and I would call. I let Jerad and Rachael go home with other friends to get them out of the waiting room.

It was about 4:00 p.m. when I was finally able to take Doug home. The doctor said to put him in bed and keep him there. He told us that Doug needed to make an appointment with his family doctor and get a CAT scan, that he may have something going on that we didn't know about that caused him to pass out like he did. Doug told him he would call the doctor on Monday and make the appointment, and we left. We drove home in silence, though I was thankful that he was ok. However, I was angry and resentful, but also ashamed for feeling that way because I could have just lost my husband. Was something wrong with me?

That night was the big Christmas Cantata at church, and, for the first time in many years, I was supposed to sing a special song. I needed to call and get someone else to sing so that I could be home that night, but Doug told me that he would be fine and that he would stay in bed. I eventually agreed to go to church and be in the cantata if he would not get up and walk around, and he agreed and promised. I arrived about forty-five minutes before the show started and was met by several concerned people who were full of questions about Doug. I told them he was fine and at home resting. I thanked them for their concern and assured them I would keep them informed.

The auditorium was dark, but I could tell through the blackness that it was full. I was nervous. I was standing on a stage in front of hundreds of people, and it had been a long time since I had done that. The fact that most of them had been in church that morning and knew what had happened with Doug was also on my mind. Would I be able to get through this without crying? My heart was full, and I felt so alone in that room of hundreds. Always alone.

The music started to play, very softly at first but just loud enough to get the attention of the crowd and indicate the show was about to begin. The choir sang, the actors were in place, and the audience sat in their seats full of joy and Christmas spirit. I anticipated my solo as it got closer; I was doing okay and prayed I would continue feeling strong to the end of the performance. Finally, it was my turn. I moved from the choir to the front of the stage, and, as I stood there singing, I could feel the emotion of the day and of the song itself well up inside of me and thought I might break into tears at any moment. I was singing about Jesus and how much He loved us, but so many times I had questioned it. If He loved me so much, why had I been given so much to deal with? I was not that strong.

Walking back to my place in the choir, I breathed a sigh of relief and wiped away a tear. I had gotten through it without falling apart. God had gotten me through it. I felt a stirring within and knew it was the Holy Spirt, the comforter. He was listening. He was there. I was not alone, and I just needed to trust Him.

That week Doug went to see his doctor and told him what had happened. The doctor scheduled the MRI and CAT Scan. I hoped they would find something to justify what had happened. As suspected, the results were normal and the collapse in church that Sunday morning would be unexplained, at least by the doctor.

One afternoon my oldest son Jerad came home from school to talk to Doug about going to look at a car that they had talked about earlier. It was an old mustang that had parts on it that Jerad needed to restore the old black Mercury that drove me to the parade so long ago. The seller told my son he needed to come get the parts that day because he was having it all hauled away. When Jerad went to the bedroom to talk to Doug, the room was pitch black as usual. The only way he was able to see Doug laying on the bed was from the light of the TV in the corner of the room. He couldn't tell if Doug was asleep, so he shook him a little—there was no response. He tried to talk to him and wake him, but that didn't work either, so he came back to the kitchen to find me. I saw the look on his face that was all too familiar; he didn't have to say a word. I knew that he and Doug would not be going to look at that car that day.

Jerad asked me if I could take him over and drop him off. He would take his tools, and if the parts were good, he would just stay and take them off the car. I drove him to the man's house and waited while they went to look under the hood of that old '82 Mustang with four flat tires still covered in dirt from the last monsoon. He came back to the car to let me know that the parts he needed looked good, and that he would stay to take them off and call me when he was finished so I could go back to pick him up.

When I returned to the house, I went back to the bedroom to check on Doug. As I walked into the dimly lit room, I saw him on the floor lying on his back, half of him in the bedroom the other half stretched into the bathroom. I froze for just a few seconds, took a deep breath, and went to the floor on my knees. I tried to wake him up but couldn't, so I checked for a pulse, expected the worst, but found one. I thanked God he was alive, once again. I looked him over to be sure he had not hurt himself, and, as far as I could tell, he hadn't. Just then my phone rang, but I let the machine pick it up. It was my son and he needed a ride home and would be waiting on the curb where I left him.

I didn't know what to do. I had to pick Jerad up, but I couldn't leave Doug alone. I ran next door to a friend and made up a story that Doug had gotten sick and laid down on the floor but had fallen asleep there. I asked her to please go over and check on him after a few minutes, and that I would be back soon. She said she would, so I got into my car and drove away.

When I got home, I went back to our room and sat there on the floor looking at this man that I didn't recognize any more and became angry. I was so angry. I was tired of always having to be the responsible one, the parent. I was tired of being afraid and of always having to worry about what was happening if I wasn't home. I finally stood up and tried to pull him off the bathroom tile and into the bedroom. At 5' 2" and 110 lbs. this was not an easy task. When I got him as far into our bedroom as I could, I grabbed the pillow off the bed, put it under his head, and shut off the bathroom light. I went into the living room and sat down on the couch with my head in my hands.

You get used to it, that's all I can say. It isn't easy to deal with, but if you can turn off the light and close the door, it's easier to take. It's like coloring your hair—the gray is there, you know it's there, but if you keep covering it up you don't notice it, and it doesn't bother you as much. Was I in denial? Yes. Did I know what to do? No. I had no idea. All I knew was I couldn't tell anyone the truth. I just couldn't. I knew this was so hard on the kids, and I tried to shield them as much as I could by making up excuses and justifying everything. They were worried and scared, and I had to keep things as normal as possible. I had to protect them, and I had to protect Doug. I didn't know how, if, or how much this was affecting our children because I didn't ask them. We didn't talk about it.

Doug's work began to suffer more and more. He wasn't teaching as often and wasn't returning phone calls. One night while I was watching TV, the phone rang in his office. I was surprised that he answered it. I heard him trying to hold a conversation with his boss, but it wasn't long into it that I realized his words were slurred, and he was not able to focus on the call. He had taken his muscle relaxers, and they had taken affect. When he got off the phone, I asked him, "Why did you answer that call?"

He said he needed to, and that his boss needed to talk to him. His slurring was worse, and I barely understood him. His eyes were heavy, and he struggled to keep them open. I was irritated and angry and told him, "You shouldn't be on the phone with your boss when you have taken those stupid pills because no one can understand what you say, and you didn't make any sense."

He didn't like what I said very much, and I didn't care very much. His boss called the next day, and I answered the phone. Just as I was about to make an excuse about why Doug couldn't come to the phone, he said he wanted to talk to me. He asked if Doug was okay and wondered if there was something that the doctor had found that Doug had not told him. I explained that after he collapsed in church that he had had the MRI and CAT scans but there was nothing to be concerned about. He mentioned the phone call from the day before and that he could hardly understand Doug on the phone. I told him that the medication the doctor had given him sometimes makes him groggy, and he had just taken one before the phone call. He was concerned but this seemed to satisfy him.

I tried to talk to Doug later that day about the call and the concern from his boss who was a genuine friend and really did care about his health. But this conversation was no different than the other countless and useless conversations about the medications and how many he was taking. It was always the same, "I take what they say I can take. Don't worry, I'm fine."

A few weeks had passed, and Doug had missed several of his classes and was canceling them as well, telling me he was not able to do it. One afternoon his boss came by to meet with him at our home. He told Doug that the company had decided that he was not reliable enough to continue working for them, and he would need to turn in all the equipment and tools that had been given to him to use in class. Doug had been fired. I was shocked but not surprised. He didn't have much to say, and, after that, he kept to himself more and more. I tried so hard to get him out of that bedroom and into the light and to be a part of our family. He was sinking, I could see it, and I had no idea what to do. He wouldn't talk about it.

What were we going to do? How were we going to make it? In tears, I cried out to God again and asked for guidance. We were not going to be able to pay our bills or rent or even buy groceries. I told a few close friends that Doug was unable to work, as they knew he had been ill. So, a few members of the church stepped up to help us, still not knowing what we were facing as a family.

I was still working for the company doing books and scheduling, but I was not bringing in enough money to support our family. Doug drew unemployment for a while until he could find something else to do. We had finally had a few serious conversations, and he knew that he was going to have to pull himself together and find another job. I was happy when he told me that he had been hired at one of the large automotive shops in the area and was going to manage two locations. The self-medicating slowed down. He knew he would not be able to work, drive, and manage these shops if he was on medication. Things were looking up again. Maybe everything was going to be okay.

CHAPTER 6

My work with Snap-on was slowing down and it felt awkward continuing to work for them after everything that had happened. After a few weeks of searching, I found a job in Scottsdale at a missionary sending agency. We soon rented and moved into a beautiful two-story home in central Gilbert. A member of our church was an investment banker and offered to buy the house we were renting. He told us that we could make rent-to-own payments to him, and it would be ours in just a few years. It was great—we had new jobs, a beautiful big house, and life was going well.

Our youngest son, Daniel, was into BMX dirt bike racing along with a friend from church. Obviously, the apple had not fallen far from the tree. The boys worked on their bikes and rode at the track every week. One night we took some friends out to the track to watch him race. Doug was excited and proud. Daniel was racing bikes just as he had. We arrived to see a crowd of parents and onlookers filling up the bleachers. We spotted some open space at the very top, and that was okay because we would be able to see better. We climbed slowly up those narrow silver bleachers to the open space at the top and sat down to enjoy a beautiful Arizona evening. A few laps in I noticed Doug had put something in his mouth. There was no question what it was, but I wasn't sure which one it was. He was still taking all the medication but had cut back on the dosage, at least during the day while working. He increased it at night when he got home but seemed to have it under control. I understood his job was causing quite a bit of pain from being on his feet all day. An hour or so passed and his words began to slur a little. Our friends, Bruce and Vicki, needed to go home, so we stood up to walk them to the car and say our goodbyes. As Doug stood up and started down the steps of the bleachers, he was so off balance he fell but was able to grab hold of a railing. I helped him up and helped him get to the bottom. Our friends offered to take him home, so that I could wait for the race to be over and get our son. It was then that the secret we had been living was out. There was no discussion, just a look that said, *we are here for you guys*. Bruce and Vicki had come to love Doug in the time that he had lived with them when arriving in Arizona. They never saw anything that told them there was a problem, until now.

As usual there were good days and bad days. On the good days we were a loving, happy, and fun family. We were very involved in our church and community. I taught Sunday school, traveled with the church Missions Team, and had a good job. I was hopeful. I knew God was with me, with us. I stayed in prayer and kept my faith; I trusted that everything was going to be okay. Was it faith or was it denial? Maybe it was a little of both.

Doug was never happy managing the shops, he wanted to be teaching. He was brilliant and knew he was wasting his time in these shops. He felt like he was moving backwards. He began looking into opportunities to teach and found one at Universal Technical Institute in Phoenix. It was a great opportunity, and things were looking up.

Doug spent quite a while teaching at UTI but was soon told by staff that the UTI in Silicon Valley, California was looking for a Director of the Automotive Department and they wanted to meet with Doug. He was so excited. This was the job and position he had worked and trained for all his life. He had finally reached the golden ring, and he wanted to grab it. This meant a move from Arizona to California, at least for him.

I was not ready to move again, at least not yet. I had left one child in Texas and didn't want to leave another in Arizona as our oldest son was graduating high school and was eighteen years old. Doug took the job with my blessing. I never wanted to be blamed for him not getting what he had worked so hard for. He was excited, full of life, and the sparkle was back in his eyes. How could I dowse that fire? We agreed that if it looked like this move was the best decision for our family, the kids and I would follow later, but for now he would go alone. He packed up his truck and drove away to follow his dream. I would now be a married single mom.

He came home every weekend for the first year. He was a completely different person. His eyes were clear, and he was full of energy. He loved what he was doing, and he loved telling us about it. The expense of coming home so often became too much. We were paying for an apartment that he shared with another instructor along with his expenses as well as the house and bills in Arizona. His salary had increased, and the pay was good, but when you are trying to keep two households going, it gets tough. Our phone calls took the place of the visits.

We had lived our lives apart before, but this was different. We were living separate lives. Our friends became my friends, our church family became my church family, our kids became my kids. Sadly, when he did come home, it could be tense. Our kids resented him disciplining or correcting them when he was home for such a short time. His self-medicating was still a problem, one that we didn't have to deal with when he was away. The days were not as bad as the nights. When he was home, he could usually be found in his recliner most of the time and pretty much unaware of what was going on around him. There would be times in the middle of the night we would hear a crash or a thud and jump up out of a sound sleep to find him on the floor and not able to walk. The truth was, in some ways, it was easier when he was away.

One Thursday evening after work, Doug called from California to tell me that he had slipped while walking through the automotive shop. He had taken a hard fall while carrying an armful of books and a cake leftover from a class party. He said he was walking and stepped on something that had been spilled on the floor. When he slipped, his feet went up in front of him, and the books went flying. Joking, he said, "But I held onto the cake!" It was German chocolate, his favorite. I laughed and ask if he was okay and he told me that he was sore, and it hurt to walk, but that he would take a day or so to rest and would be fine.

On Monday he was no better, so he found a doctor that would see him and made an appointment to get checked out. The doctor examined him and sent him for x-rays. When the results came back, he was sent to a specialist as he had damaged some lower vertebrate. He was immediately put on workman's comp and would not be able to work for a while. The semester was almost over, and someone else would finish up his class. Doug called his insurance company and asked if he would be able to see a doctor in Arizona to recover. After getting everything approved, he loaded up his truck and came home.

The injury to his back was more than we realized. I watched as he walked into the house, and it was as if I were looking at an eighty-year-old man. He greeted me with a big smile and a happy-to-see-you hello, but I could tell that he was in pain. The drive from California took a toll on him even though he stopped several times to stretch. He was glad to be home and ready to sit in his favorite chair. The big black leather recliner sat facing the television exactly where he left it, and he gently lowered himself into the comfort of its arms.

Workman's Compensation required Doug to go see our family doctor once a month and requested a form be filled out each time to show that he was getting medical care. Being our family doctor, he had treated Doug before and was aware of his medical history. It was also nice that I knew he and his wife personally from my job. I had worked with them and their church on mission planning. The doctor was going to have to treat Doug's new injury and document treatment that was required. He would also have to find a specialist that workman's compensation would approve of in our area and schedule an appointment for Doug. In the meantime, there would be more prescriptions written to control the pain.

It was 2002, and we were a family again. I had missed it. I was glad I didn't have to be a single parent anymore. The doctor had ordered an MRI. He wasn't sure if surgery was going to be needed until some of the swelling had gone down and they could get a better look at the discs. Of course, Doug already had back pain from the surgery a few years earlier, and this was making those issues even worse. Doug was on his own during the day but spent most of his time downstairs in his recliner. Navigating the stairs was not easy and not something I wanted him to do when he was alone. Those early days were spent reading and sleeping. He read all the time, articles about the automotive industry—what was new and what was coming. He was always reading, learning, and studying. He went to the doctor regularly as he was instructed to do and took the medications that were given to him.

We began to teach an adult Sunday school class, and it was nice spending time studying the material together and reading the Bible. We had been through a lot. I knew God was there all along, but sometimes my faith was a little shaken. I kept telling myself that God would never give me more than He knew I could handle, but there were times that I thought He had given me too much credit. God had seen me through so many things in my life, and I knew He wouldn't leave me. I had faith that things were going to be fine.

Our oldest daughter was still in Texas, married with two children. Our oldest son was on his own but lived nearby. The two youngest were both in high school. My job was about a 45-minute commute on a good day. My mom was battling cancer back in Texas, and I called her every morning on the way to work to pass the time during the commute. I flew back to Texas as often as I could, usually every four months or so and would be gone for a long weekend. One of those times I was at the oncologist with her while she was getting a chemo treatment. It was a long slow process, so I took a break and went outside to call home. We were having new flooring installed in our house, and I wanted to see how it was going. I called several times, and no one answered the phone. Finally, Doug picked up. I asked him if the flooring guys had shown up and had the work been started? He mumbled something, and I couldn't understand him. He managed to tell me that the workers were there but little else. Frustrated, not being able to find out what was going on, I told him to give the phone to one of the kids. In a few minutes a man's voice said, "Hello."

I asked, "Who is this?

He said, "This is Raul, the contractor."

"Is everything okay?" I asked.

"There is something wrong with the señor."

He said that Doug had let them in and was stumbling everywhere and could barely stand. He also said that when he tried to speak with him about the work, he couldn't understand Doug at all. I explained that he had a fall and an injury, and the medication was causing it.

I answered his questions about the work, and I told him to proceed. I gave him my cell number along with my parents' phone number and told him to call me when he needed something. He told me it was going to take a couple of days to complete the job. I explained I would not be there, and he needed to be sure to keep in contact with me.

Here I was outside the oncology office pacing with my cell phone trying to take care of a situation 900 miles away while my mother was inside hooked up to a drip fighting for her life. I was confused and concerned, but most of all I was angry. How had my life gotten to this point? How was I was going to get through all of this? How were my kids going to get through this? My kids—they were there dealing with this situation while I was here, then the guilt kicked in. I was on the phone over the next couple of days regularly with them making sure they were okay and that they had food and were managing without me. They, of course, reassured me that they were fine, and everything was okay. Unfortunately, this scenario would play out again.

My mom was having a hard time, and I was an only child, so I had to do what I could to help. How was I going to do that with my own life in shambles? I talked to the kids and to Doug about the situation. They all agreed that I needed to be with my mother. I spoke at length to Doug in private about what happens when I'm gone. I told him how much I worry because I didn't know if I could trust him to take care of the kids. He nodded, and he assured me that he would monitor his medications and that he and the kids would be fine. My parents needed me, so go!

This time I was at my parents' house when my phone rang. It was Doug telling me he was in the hospital. I found out from a nurse that the gas man was going by each house to say the gas was going to be shut off for a little while, and when Doug answered the door, he was incoherent and literally foaming from the mouth. The man was so scared he called 911 and the paramedics came. What was happening? Where are my kids? After a few tries, I reached them on the phone, they were fine— worried, but fine.

While on my phone trying to figure out solutions for what was going on in Arizona, I paced in my parents' back yard. Panic, fear, worry, guilt, and anger filled my heart and mind. I began to walk and pray and walk some more. My dad came out a couple of times asking if everything was okay. I said it was, and he went back inside. I wasn't going to let them know what was happening, what we were dealing with, and what our lives had become. They had enough to worry about with mom and the cancer. All I could do was talk to myself and to God and ask: What is wrong with Doug? What can I do?

I worried about my kids—what was this doing to them? They should not have to be responsible to look after their dad. I kept telling myself that I was a bad mother. That I should be there taking care of this. Standing in my parents' back yard, I cried out to God, "I can't do this anymore. I can't handle it anymore. Please show me what to do. Help me!" Crying out to God and praying was all I could do at that moment. Doug was treated for an overdose and sent home. I was on the next plane back to Arizona.

Looking back on the events I wish I had shared my struggles sooner and gotten advice, guidance, and help. At the time this was taking place, opioid abuse was not widely discussed. I had no idea what I was dealing with, let alone how to deal with it.

As much as I hated leaving home, my trips back to Texas were ongoing and not without incident. On yet another occasion, I called home to check on things, and I found out that Doug had driven himself to Tucson and was unable to get home, so he called our sixteen-year-old daughter who had just gotten her license to come pick him up. When she told me this, I freaked out and forbid her to go. I told her to call her older brother and explain what was going on and tell him I needed him to make the drive and get Doug home.

When I returned to Arizona, I confronted Doug about this. He told me he went to look at a car that he was thinking about buying but couldn't explain why he was not able to drive himself back to Phoenix, although I already knew the answer. I would later find out that he had gone to the Nogales border to buy pain meds.

The addiction was serious, and he was going through his prescriptions so quickly that he had to find another way to get them. Opioid addiction was not as prevalent then as it is now, or maybe it just wasn't as newsworthy unless you happened to be a movie star. This was out of my control, no matter how hard I fought him, warned him, threatened him, begged him, and cried, it was useless. His answer never wavered, "I'm fine."

I was lost. I had no idea how to help him or any of us. I had no information on support groups or even how to find information had I known about them. Sure, I had heard of AA and Al-Anon, but that was for alcoholics, right?

Since my trips to Texas were always eventful at home, I could not trust Doug to be "present" while I was away, and I didn't want to leave my kids to shoulder that responsibility. The man I would have trusted with my life, was no longer trustworthy. There were so many lies, so many times that I found drugs hidden around the house, and so many times he let me down when I needed him. When I looked at him, I saw him through angry eyes. I no longer saw the strong, handsome man that swept me off my feet and promised to take care of me forever. He was gone, and in his place was someone that had given up and seemed not to or unable to care.

Although Doug was still going to church with us most of time, that too would end. No matter how many times I begged him not to take any of the drugs before we went to church, he would anyway. He would promise not to, but he rarely kept that promise. We would be in church, and before the sermon was halfway through, he was hardly able to keep his head up. It wobbled back and forth, and I would punch him or pinch him to get him to stop. Eventually he stopped going. It was easier that way for all of us. Because he was no longer a part of teaching the couples Sunday School class, I had to let it go so that another couple could lead it. I understood but I resented it, just another thing I had to give up because of his addiction. It wasn't long before I had to resign as Missions Director at the church because I was no longer able to lead the Mexico trips. Though I had been a summer missionary to Mexico for years, I was no longer going to be able to serve in that capacity. My Mexico Mission work was one of the bright places in my life and something I felt called to do, but now it would have to be set aside. This was heartbreaking.

I asked God on several occasions: Why? God, if you are there, and you really do care about me, do something! Do something! Many times, I would literally say out loud, "I don't know. I don't know. I can't. I can't." because no other words would come. I was living a lie. I had learned to put on a good show, but behind closed doors, my life was a mess and I was losing faith.

My time was spent at work or at home with little in between, and I became resentful. I felt myself becoming more and more bitter and angry with this man that I had once adored. I was angry because he disappeared, and I couldn't find him. On occasion I would get a glimpse of him and realize just how much I missed him.

I was in a battle against a monster much larger than me, and I was running out of strength to fight. I was losing. I had nowhere else to turn, and I felt that my prayers were not being heard and so, I called my pastor. I told him the whole ugly story and the secret I had been keeping for such a long time. I needed help.

Pastor Larry and I scheduled a time for him to come over and do an intervention. I told Doug that he was coming but didn't tell him why I asked him not to take any meds before our pastor got here. When he arrived, we went into our home office. It was dimly lit, and there was a large, empty desk— that used to be where Doug worked— and three chairs set in a circle. The conversation was small talk at first, then Pastor Larry asked Doug some questions about his injury and his medications. Pastor Larry asked if Doug had considered going to a pain clinic, or to a rehab? He offered to help us find a place close by. Doug nodded and said he would think about it. It was obvious he had taken something because he was fading. The meds were kicking in, and we were losing him.

Pastor Larry said goodbye and I walked him to the door. He hugged me and said, "He needs help but until he admits that, he won't get it." He told me to call him anytime I needed him. I knew there was nothing he could do for Doug except pray, and I knew that was true for me as well. I finally admitted to myself that the man with the bright blue eyes where his spirit shone through was an addict and the light was going out. I began to read about addiction, and the literature always ended with the same thing that pastor Larry had said. An addict will not get help until he can admit his addiction and ask for it. What was I going to do? I had no knowledge, no experience, and no resources. I felt so alone.

There were times when Doug would be almost comatose sitting in his chair or lying on the bed. Most times getting a response from him was difficult. The kids and I had grown accustomed to the sound of furniture being bumped, breaking glass, thuds on the floor, and slipping on the stairs. One night I heard him downstairs. I went down to see what he was doing, and I found him standing in the kitchen with a screwdriver and our toaster. He said he had taken it apart because it wasn't working—it was still plugged into the wall. On another night I found him in our bathroom taking the blow dryer apart for the same reason. Somewhere in his mind he still had the need to make things better, to get them to work because they were broken. Why couldn't he see how broken he was?

43

So many times, we would rush to pick him up off the floor, put him in his chair or back in bed. It was just a part of our lives. There was a day when one of my children had friends over and Doug was upstairs. He got down the stairs to the kitchen and stumbled over everything in his path and was barely able to speak. He made his way back to the stairs and to our room. I am not sure what happened in that kitchen, but my child came to me and said, "Mom, please keep daddy up there." It broke my heart. What was happening to my family? My children were being affected. and I couldn't stop it. No matter how hard I tried, I couldn't fix it. A mother is supposed to protect her kids and make things right. I couldn't, and I was devastated. What kind of mother was I? I was blessed with these children, and I was letting them down. I was supposed to protect them, and I wasn't. They shouldn't have had to grow up with this. They shouldn't have had to see this every day.

I should have gotten counseling; I should have taken my kids to counseling. I ask myself and others have asked me why I didn't. The answer is, I don't know. In my denial, I just kept telling myself that they would be okay, and Doug would all be okay. If there were resources out there, I had no idea how to find them.

One day, after a discussion with my two youngest who were still at home and enduring some very difficult days, we decided to try and get through to Doug to make him see what he was doing to himself and to his family. Another intervention. We went upstairs to the bedroom, it was dark as usual, the TV was on in the corner of the room, but the volume was down very low. He was lying on our bed on his back wearing his usual black t-shirt and cut off shorts. As we entered the room, I turned on the light and he turned to see the three of us standing next to him. I said, "We want to talk to you."

Looking down at him and struggling not to cry I asked, "Do you want to die?"

He looked at me so strangely, and for a minute I recognized the man I married—he was lucid and present.

He said "No, I don't want to die."

I told him that if he kept going like he had been he would die and nothing we could do would prevent that. I told him that until he admitted that he had a problem with the drugs and got help he was taking his life into his own hands. The kids begged him to stop. They were so strong, so forceful, yet spoke with so much love for their dad. The love was still there, but the trust and the respect had gone. He told us how much he loved us and that he would do better. He didn't say that he had a problem, and he didn't say he needed help. He didn't see it or didn't want to. Nothing changed; it would only get worse.

Doug was taking himself to his doctor appointments; arguing with me that he wasn't helpless. One day, on the way to or from an appointment, he was pulled over by a police officer for weaving. He somehow was able to convince the officer he was just tired and was sent on his way. I know this because I found the warning ticket he was given.

Another time I showed up at a doctor appointment without telling him and confronted the doctor. Any time in the past that I went with Doug to the doctor and mentioned that he was taking too much, and he was sleeping too much they would question him, and he would not admit to it. They did not or could not do anything but explain the dosage and remind him to take it only as prescribed. Doug would agree and admit to occasionally taking an extra dose here or there if he was hurting worse than usual. This time I was angry, and they were going to listen to me. I knew they didn't know the whole story, or, if they did, they didn't care. I explained what was going on in our home and that I thought he was being given too many meds. So, the doctor (working directly with workman's comp and disability) immediately said, "He must be having a reaction to them. Let's change it up a little and that will probably take care of it." It was as if I hadn't said a thing. The meds kept coming and no one was listening.

Doug was hiding pills everywhere in the house and in the garage. He would tell me he didn't have any or was out and then be unresponsive in his chair or our room. I was constantly searching, and when I found hidden pills, I threw them away. No more excuse, no more listening, no more believing. I was in a bad place. I had gotten to the point of not caring. It was now becoming resentment. I felt myself changing; I felt myself slipping away. Why should I care, why should I? He doesn't.

One day I found him on the floor in the kitchen. He was having a seizure, shaking violently, so I called 911. The paramedics came and rushed him to the emergency room. The nurse asked me about the meds he was on and how often he took them. I told her the truth about everything. They gave him an injection to counter the overdose and kept him for observation for a few hours. When he was able to communicate and understand, the doctor came in, and he and the nurse spoke to Doug about getting help. They explained that there was help available and they could call and get it started right away. The doctor explained how close of a call he had just had. He told Doug that if he didn't get help and continued down this road that he would die. Doug said thank you, he was okay but took the information with him. There was nothing they or I could do.

This was the first and only time a medical professional had heard me, listened to me, and believed me. I spoke up, I told the truth, and I asked for help. I begged Doug to take it, but he didn't. The answer was right there in front of us, and he didn't take it. I drove him home in silence and disappointment.

CHAPTER 7

A few weeks later my son had several friends over. Some of them hovered in front of the TV in the family room, and some kept going in and out of the back door making all sorts of rackets. Because Doug was upstairs in "the cave" as I had begun to call our bedroom, I didn't have a place to go to find a quiet moment. I walked down the hall and through the laundry room and heard the rumble of the dryer running with the final load. I walked into the garage that smelled like boys, where bicycles were turned upside down and tools lay on the ground along with red rags and empty soda cans.

I opened my car door and climbed in. The silence was deafening. I leaned back in my seat and closed my eyes and thought about how much my life had changed, how I felt so defeated. Tears began to fall as I realized I was reaching my breaking point. Without saying a word to anyone, I started the car and took a drive. I had no destination; I didn't even have my purse. I just drove and pulled into a parking lot and sobbed.

When I returned home, I sat in the car for a while, and then the laundry room door opened, and I saw my son Daniel walking toward me. As he walked to the car and looked at me, I rolled the window down and he asked, "What are you doing mom, where were you?" As I looked into his blue eyes that were so much his father's eyes, they began to well up with tears. He said, "Mom, I wasn't sure you were coming back. Please don't leave us."

I couldn't believe what I heard. I remember the feeling I felt and being reminded once again how much my children needed me. I looked at that face and said, "I won't, I promise."

Was this coincidence? I doubt it. I know it was God reminding me that my work was not done. There was more I had to do, and my children were going to need me now more than ever. I just didn't know why.

So many more times I would find Doug incoherent. It became a way of life. It was my life. It was our life. One night, I came home from work and went up to our room to change my clothes. He was in the usual place in the usual position—on the bed, on his back, in a dark room. I called to him to let him know I was home, but there was no response. I walked over to the bed and shook him; he fluttered his eyes as was the norm and I knew he was okay, so I turned to walk away. As I did, I noticed a small red light coming from underneath him on one side. I walked over and rolled him a bit to find a massage wand that he had placed under his shoulder at some point to relieve pain and fell asleep. I noticed a smell as I pulled the device from under him, I reached over to the bedside table and turned on the lamp. I rolled him over a bit to look at his back and saw that the machine had gotten so hot that it not only burned a spot on the sheet, but it had burned his back deeply. I tried to wake him, but I couldn't, so I went to the first aid kit and cleaned and dressed the wound as best I could. He never felt a thing.

I was so angry, and when he came to, I yelled, "You could have set the house on fire. You could have burned up with it and never have been aware of it. What is wrong with you?" That burn was serious and would leave a terrible scar. Another time I found him in the bathtub, completely out of it and only inches from drowning. I knew that if this were ever going to change, God would have to do it.

Money was tight. His workman's comp was running out, and my job didn't pay enough to make much difference. We were behind on our house payments, and even though I tried to explain the situation without being completely honest, I fell further and further behind. Because I didn't want to worry the kids, I knew I would have to get a second job or something to pay the bills. I was isolated and broken. I had no one to talk to and no one to share my distress. I only had God, and I was starting to feel that He wasn't listening.

In October of 2003, I got a call from a family member in Texas telling me that my mom had taken a turn and I needed to get to Amarillo. I remembered all the other times I had gone to Texas and left my kids alone with their dad. I remembered everything that happened, and I didn't know what to do. I talked to my kids, and I talked to my oldest son and told him I needed him to watch over the kids and Doug as best he could. I didn't know what I would find in Texas, and I didn't know how long I would be gone. When I got there, I could see that her time was not long for this world, so I told all four kids and Doug that they needed to get there as fast as they could. They were able to get there in time to say goodbye, and I was glad.

I lost my mom to cancer. I was hurting, and I was broken, and even during the most horrible time in my life, I couldn't depend on my husband to be there for me because along with his arrival came the mistress. The mistress of addiction. He couldn't leave her behind. I couldn't fight her; I couldn't offer him what she could. I couldn't give him what he felt he needed. In my pain and despair, I wrote this:

> *She creeped in amidst the darkness, like a fog consumes the sky*
> *To her victims she was nameless, and I didn't really try*
> *Her importance to me was unclear, so my attention was distracted*
> *Although I knew when she was near, her power not yet detected*
> *In time her presence I questioned, and how often she appeared*
> *In response I suggested, one that he didn't want to hear*
> *I requested he decide, a choice between her and me*
> *He asked that I see his position, "There's no problem here I see"*
> *"You're wrong about her power, I just need her now and again"*
> *"Her voice is never louder, than the voice I have within"*
> *I knew she'd won the battle, her control much stronger than mine*
> *Up a creek without a paddle, it was only a matter of time*
> *I remember the day he left me, how suddenly it came*
> *Her grip was never ceasing, by now I knew her name*
> *Her name is now important, as I look back onto the past*
> *Her name will not lie dormant, in my life it will forever last*
> *She lives in many households, her grasp has no restriction*
> *In time she gains control, and I know her as addiction.*

After the funeral and making sure my daddy was okay, I returned home to Arizona and my life. Weeks later I would find myself sitting in a parking lot of a convenience store collapsed on my steering wheel with tears running down my face. I was going home to tell my husband that after twenty years I was done. I was going to pack his bag, call his mother, and put him on a plane back to Levelland. I was going to give him the ultimatum: either he gets help when he is there, or he couldn't come back. We were through. The man I loved so much and trusted with my life was gone and someone else had taken his place. I called my pastor and told him what I was going to do. We prayed together on the phone, and I dried my tears and drove three blocks to my house.

A few minutes later, I got a call from my oldest daughter telling me that her marriage had fallen apart, and her husband had decided he didn't want to be married to her anymore. She was devastated and didn't know what to do. It was ironic when she told me how alone she felt. I told her not to worry and to pack up her things and my two grandchildren and move to Arizona to be close to her family. My conversation with Doug would have to wait. We worked out the details and began preparing the house for their arrival. I needed to help her; I never wanted her to feel she was alone.

After everything was in place and she had arranged the move, we planned for her arrival on Friday, February 6, 2004. Everything was ready for them, and I was looking forward to having all my kids and grandkids close by. We would all be together again.

That week I had been sleeping in the downstairs bedroom that had been cleaned out for my grandson to use when they arrived from Texas. Doug was up and down out of bed every night, wandering or rummaging, so it was easier to sleep away from him. It had been a long time since I had slept through the night. I was always listening for Doug to get up, or possibly fall. Sleeping alone in a separate room was hard at first but soon the exhaustion took over and I fell asleep. At some point I began to dream about my mom; I had been missing her so much. I can't say for sure if I was dreaming or if it really happened, but my eyes opened, and, standing in the darkness in front of the closed bedroom door, I saw my mom. She was beautiful, and she looked so healthy. She smiled at me and said, "I know this is hard, but everything is going to be okay. You are going to be okay. I love you." Then she was gone.

When I sat up in bed, I was crying. I was sad, but I felt so calm and at peace, and I had not felt like that in a very long time. I lay down, closed my eyes and drifted into a restful and peaceful sleep.

Like any other morning, I had gotten up that Wednesday to get ready for the day. I went into the rooms of my two teenage children still in bed with covers pulled up to their necks and nudged them to get ready for school. A slight stirring from under the covers only caused them to bury themselves deeper into the mound of blankets. I walked down the stairs to the kitchen and noticed a few soda cans on the counter, half full as usual. As I mumbled under my breath about the waste, I emptied them into the sink. I pulled the cord on the shades letting the morning make its way in and found the coffee pot full of fresh brewed coffee just waiting for a little cream and sugar. I grabbed my cup and made my way into the living room where I found the remote buried under the couch cushions and turned on the morning news. Since it was a workday and I had a big meeting to prepare for, I did not have a lot of time to sit and watch.

I took my coffee and headed back upstairs, avoiding the obstacle course of laundry baskets I had set on the steps for the kids to take to their rooms. Walking down the upstairs hall to our bedroom, I called to my kids to get up and get ready for school before I closed the door.

As I walked into our bedroom, I noticed the bed was really messed up. The blankets were on the floor and the sheets were barely hanging on to the mattress. The room was dark as usual, the blinds were down, and the curtains drawn tight so not an ounce of light could peep through. The television was on but muted, and my husband was lying in the middle of the bed flat on his back. He didn't notice the shower running or the kids yelling at each other in the hall to hurry up and get out of the bathroom either. I glanced at him while I fumbled in the dark to find clothing in the dresser drawers. I hated the dark and wished I could flip on the light.

As I was leaving the room, I stopped next to him after noticing that he hadn't moved from the position he was in when I first came into the room. He was still lying on his back with the pillow off to one side. He lay very still, so I moved closer to watch him breathe, watching for life. I panicked and shook him, but there was no response. Then I shook him much harder which caused him to stir and flutter his eyes. He was not completely responsive, so I climbed on the bed, straddled him and began to shake him until his eyes finally opened. First, they opened only slightly and then I saw his beautiful, crystal blue eyes looking at me, confused. "Are you okay?"

51

He said, "Yes, what's wrong?"

He started to drift again, so I shook him harder and asked, "Are you sure you are okay?"

He responded again, "Yes, what's wrong? Is something wrong?"

I said, "No, I just needed to be sure you were okay before I left for work." I told him I had a very important meeting, but that I would call him when I got to the office. He nodded and closed his eyes. As I walked down the hall, I stopped at my daughter's door and told her to check on her dad before she left for school, that he was having a bad morning. She knew all too well what that meant. She asked me if he was okay and should she stay home. I told her no, he was fine, and she should go to school.

About 11:30 a.m., my cell phone rang just as I walked into the meeting. The voice on the other end was young and scared, it was my daughter, Rachael. "Mom, something's wrong with Daddy. He is laying on the floor, and I don't think he's breathing." The feeling that came over me was just as I expected it would be, as if the world stopped for just that moment, just long enough for my heart to stop beating.

I took a breath, and as that breath came, so did the words, "Do you feel a heartbeat? See if there is a heartbeat. Put your hand on his chest or feel for a pulse. See if you can feel his heart beating." I heard the phone hit the table, and then there was silence for a few minutes. It seemed like forever until I heard her voice again. I was already prepared to hear what she would say; I had played it in my head so many times.

"No mom, he is so cold, and I can't move his hands."

I closed my eyes. Tears began to fall as I told my daughter, "Hang up the phone and call 911. I'm on my way."

I turned to my boss who was standing in the conference room with others gathered for this meeting. He could tell by my expression that something was wrong. I hurriedly grabbed my purse and walked towards him. As he met me at the door, I said as calmly as I could without complete hysteria, "I have to go, there is something wrong with my husband, and I have to get home."

"Terrie, what's happened, what can we do?"

"Nothing, I just have to go, and I don't have time to talk." I turned and quickly ran to the door with him and others following behind me.

"Let us drive you. You don't need to drive."

"I'm fine, I will be fine. I will let you know what's happening later."

I got to my car and I climbed inside with my cell phone in hand, and, as I drove, I called friends to tell them I needed help. I called my church and Patty answered, "Patty, I need you to find Pastor Larry and get him to my house right now. Something has happened to Doug, and Rachael is alone at the house. I need someone there with her."

Patty started to ask questions, but I cut her off. "Patty, I have to go, I'm driving, and I am on my way home now."

Just before I hung up, I heard her say, "Terrie stop the car, pull over, let me come and get you."

"No, I'm on my way. Get to Rachael."

I hung up and called two of my friends, Vicki and Kathy. I told them there was something wrong with Doug, Rachael was alone, and Pastor Larry was on his way. I asked them to please get to the house and be with Rachael. I don't remember making the drive, but I do remember praying over and over that Doug was okay and that Rachael was not alone.

Our house was the second one from the corner, and as I turned onto our street, I could see an ambulance, police cars, and people standing in front of their homes and in front of mine. I couldn't get to my driveway. I remember jumping the curb and pulling up into our yard. As I got out of the car I began to run toward the house and was met by the police. There were others there as well, but I can't tell you who. I felt hands take hold of me and a voice saying that Doug was gone. I fell to my knees in the front yard and cried out, "No, No, No, it's my fault. I should have never left him."

I remember voices saying it wasn't my fault, and helping me to my feet, holding me and walking me to my front door. I got control of myself and yelled out, "Where's Rachael, where's Rachael?"

They told me she was inside and led me into my living room, full of police officers and friends. There in that room I saw my daughter, her face drained of color and drenched in tears. She ran to me and I grabbed hold of her and held on as tightly as I could. In a soft voice she struggled to say, "Mom, Daddy is gone. He's gone."

Through tears of my own I said, "I know sweetie."

I wanted to go upstairs. I wanted to get to Doug. The police had the stairs and the area around the stairs taped off. It looked like a crime scene. I cried and begged them to let me go up there, but they told me it was an investigation, and I couldn't go up there until it had been cleared. I didn't understand, and I was too emotional to try. One of the officers came to me and explained that because Doug had apparently died alone, and no one was present at the time, they would have to do some investigating and would need to ask some questions when I was ready.

I know I had conversations with the wonderful friends that came to the house. I know they reassured me of how much they loved us and would be there for us, but I don't remember it. I remember saying I had to tell the other kids. Someone asked me where Daniel was, and I told them he was at school. They told me not to worry; they would go to the school and get him. I needed to call Jerad, but he was working, and I didn't have or couldn't think of how to reach him. I called his girlfriend and told her what had happened and that I needed her to find Jerad and tell him to get to the house. I knew I had to call Erika, who was in the middle of packing up to move to Arizona and tell her. When I called, she answered, sounding very tired and stressed from packing. I said, "Erika, something has happened. Doug is gone. He passed away."

"What? What happened? I'm on my way."

"No, it's okay. Just finish what you need to do there and leave as planned."

We argued a bit as she wanted to be here with the family. I convinced her there was nothing she could do, and we would wait to plan the funeral until she got here.

An officer approached me and asked if we could sit down and talk for a minute. We sat at our dining room table away from the others in the house. He explained that he needed to ask me some questions and that he would need to ask Daniel and Rachael questions as well. He asked for my permission and I agreed.

"Mrs. Durham, when was the last time you saw your husband?"

"This morning, before I left for work."

"What time was that?"

"Around 7:15."

"Was he okay when you last saw him?"

"Yes. No. He has been sick."

"Mrs. Durham, when you arrived today, you said that it was your fault. Can you explain what you meant?"

I began to explain that Doug had a problem with pain medication and that he often took too many. I told him that there were many times that he would just not be responsive to us. I told him about the overdoses and the hospital visits and that this was something we dealt with daily. I said, "This morning he was having a bad morning, I could tell that he had taken too many pills and was very groggy. I was able to get a response out of him, and he seemed to be okay. I thought he would be because he is always okay. I asked my daughter to check on him before she went to school. She did. He was out of it, but that was normal. I should never have left him; I should have stayed home and been here with him."

"This was normal behavior for him?"

"Yes."

"You didn't see anything that was out of the norm?"

"No, he talked to me. He answered me."

"Okay, it's okay." He reached over and patted my hand. He said that was all he needed and that he would speak to Daniel and Rachael because they were the last ones to see him that morning.

Soon my son Jerad arrived. He came bursting into the house yelling for me. I tried to calm him down and hold him, but he was too upset. He wanted to know what happened. I explained about the morning and that it was no different than any other day. He wanted to go upstairs, but the officers stopped him. Jerad was agitated and forceful and said, "I want to see my dad. Let me go see him."

The officers held him back and explained why they couldn't let us go up there yet, but as soon as the investigation was over, we would be able to.

It had been hours, and finally the officer came to me and said that if we wanted to go up, we could because the investigation was over, and they would be removing his body in a few minutes. Daniel did not want to go, and that was okay. I remember looking at his face and seeing such pain and sorrow. He looked so much like his dad, but today he looked broken.

Jerad, Rachael, and I slowly walked upstairs to my bedroom. As I walked in, I could see officers standing around. I looked on the bed expecting to see Doug because that is where I had left him. He wasn't there. The lights were all on, the blinds were opened, and the room saw light that it hadn't in quite some time. A few steps in I saw my husband lying on the floor at the foot of our bed. He was lying on his back with a blanket covering his lower body. We walked closer and knelt next to him. Jerad was shaking, the young man that was always so strong and in control was crying as he reached for his dad's hand. I looked at the face of the man I had married so many years before and remembered that day, and all the other good days we had together. I leaned over him and looked into his beautiful blue eyes that I loved so much and saw that the shine was now gone, that light had gone out. I bent down and whispered, "You're okay now, no more pain."

I kissed his lips, so cold and blue and said, "I love you."

Had I said it that morning? I couldn't remember.

CHAPTER 8

My husband died that day, February 4, 2004, due to an accidental drug overdose of prescription medications. He was forty-eight years old. He left behind a wife, four children, and five grandchildren. In the days ahead I felt many emotions. I was heartbroken of course, and I was angry. I was so angry that he had left us, that he had left me. There were nights when I was alone when I questioned his love for me. If he had loved me, he would have gotten help, he would still be here.

This is a letter I wrote to Doug several weeks after his death:

> *Doug, I want to be sure you know that I loved you very much. I tried for so long to get you to see how harmful the drugs you were taking were. So many years I watched you ever so slowly kill the man I loved. There were times I begged you to stop and to get help, sometimes in tears and other times in anger. You never heard me, and you never heard our children. I understand more about addiction now, and I know it was an illness but, I am still angry with you. I am angry because along with your own life you took away mine. Your addiction consumed my life, you consumed my life, and then you left me to pick up the pieces.*
>
> *We both now have peace. I will always love you.*
>
> *Forever, Your Darlin.*

A few months after he passed away, I went out to my car to look for a small tape recorder that I had been using. For some reason I turned it on and heard a familiar voice that took me by surprise, and as I listened, tears filled my eyes. The voice of my husband said, "Darlin, I just need you to know how much I love you."

I had been so angry and resentful for so long that I couldn't see the love anymore. I was angry and hurt that he left me, and I had convinced myself that he didn't care. The truth was he did care. He loved me, and he loved his family very much. I needed to hear those words, I needed to be reminded that the man I fell in love with never stopped loving me, never stopped thinking about me.

I sat in the car for a while thinking about who we used to be together. That young man that introduced me to his mother and said, "What do you think mom? They just keep getting better."

I laughed and thought about things that I had not thought of in years. I thought about how he loved the *Alien* movies with Sigourney Weaver. How he would put his hand over the face of our kids and grandkids and make his version of an alien sound sucking their faces. I thought about him in our backyard with our grandson Bailey. Doug would hang onto the handles of his stroller revving the engine, then pretending it was a dragster, on the start, getting warmed up. I remembered ice cream in bed and peanut M&M's, Dr Pepper, and Cheetos. And as I remembered, I smiled, while tears ran down my face. I missed him.

My husband left this world of pain and woke up in heaven standing before our Heavenly Father. He is strong again. He is well. I like to think he is behind the wheel of a dragster shooting through the clouds faster than he had ever gone before.

What could I have done differently, what didn't I do? I carried the guilt and blame for years. Since the day Doug lost his life, my family has not talked about the addiction. It's as if we put it in a box and taped it up. I think we were protecting each other; I think we still are. There was one occasion when my son Jerad and I were talking about Doug and he looked at me and said, "We didn't do enough."

Maybe we didn't, maybe I didn't. I don't know. What I do know, is that I loved him fiercely and missed him desperately.

While planning the funeral I decided that I wanted to do the eulogy. I ended it by saying, "He was a very good man." And he was.

After the funeral, I was approached by a family friend who said, "That's what's important, to be a good man. I hope someone says that about me when my time comes."

Good men, good women, and good children struggle with things every day. Those struggles do not make them bad people. The struggles, though, sometimes cause them to make bad decisions. Addiction comes in all forms and affects families from all walks of life: the rich and famous, the blue-collar workers, and the church-going Christians. Because opioid addiction was not widely discussed all those years ago, my options for help were not clear. Today, addiction is widespread and, fortunately, the options for help are more available.

I want to encourage those that are walking a difficult journey, whether it is addiction, financial hardship, loss, or illness to talk to someone. I wish I would have searched out a support group or an agency that would have helped me and my family. I wish I would have realized that it was not an embarrassment but an opportunity to know other people who struggle with the same kind of issues. I wish someone had told me I was an enabler.

The decision not to share with friends or family was my choice, and it was wrong. I thought I was protecting my family. I didn't want anyone to judge Doug or think badly of him. Writing this book was difficult in many ways, one of the things I didn't want to do was to make Doug look bad to other people. I guess in a way I was still protecting him. It took several years for me to be able to tell this story. At great cost, I learned that addiction is not an embarrassment; it is a disease.

If you are living with addiction, or with someone with an addiction, you know every one of these feelings firsthand. You may know what you need to do, but perhaps are unable to do it. Maybe it is because you don't see a way to survive financially; maybe it's because you don't want to upset the family, the children; maybe it's because you don't want to admit failure. Whatever the reasons, they are valid, but not asking for help because of them is the wrong choice.

CHAPTER 9

Am I to blame for my husband's death? I used to think so. I can tell you that I have released that blame. I have forgiven him, and I have forgiven myself. It is by the grace of God that I can tell this story and that I am certain I will one day see Doug again in Heaven.

There is a quote I heard many years ago by a man named William Stafford just before he died. He said, *"There is a thread you follow. It goes among things that change but, it doesn't change. People wonder about what you are pursuing. You must explain about the thread. But it's hard for others to see. While you hold it, you can't get lost. Tragedies happen; people get hurt or die; and you suffer and get old. Nothing you do can stop times unfolding. You don't ever let go of the thread."*

To me, this thread is God who lives in me. Though the people, circumstances, situations, and choices in my life will continue to change, the thread will never change. God will remain living and breathing in me. He is the thread that remains intact, binding, never breaking.

The God I serve is always wrapped around my heart, leading and guiding. Even through the sharp edges of life may throw themselves in my path, my God holds strong and I remain strong in Him.

Even though I felt alone so many times, I wasn't. My relationship with Jesus sustained me. Being a Christian, a "believer," does not mean that we will not go through hard things in our lives, because we will. The promise is that we will never go through them alone.

Jesus has walked with me through every day of my life. He never gave up on me. Though there have been times when I tried to walk ahead of Him or away from Him, His love for me never changed. Although I have walked through the fire, my refinement is not over. I still have a lot of growing to do.

When I am asked why I want to share this story with the world, I tell people that this is my testimony. My life has taken many twists and turns, I have survived struggles and hardship, but this tragedy, this landslide, almost took me down. When I felt the ground crumble, saw my world collapse and I was going down, I reached up and took the hand of God.

This book is titled Landslide from a song that spoke volumes to me during a very difficult time in my life, Landslide by Stevie Nicks/Fleetwood Mac. The song talks about changes and the ability to make them and survive them. I had built my life around my family and had put so much focus on protecting them. My husband was gone, my children were getting older and would soon be gone and I was getting older too. What would my life be now? Would I be able to make it on my own?

John 16:32 A time is coming and in fact has come when you will be scattered, each to your own home. You will leave me all alone. Yet I am not alone, for my Father is with me.

AFTERWORD:

Opioids are substances that work in the nervous system of the body or in specific receptors in the brain to reduce the intensity of pain.

Prescription opioids can be used to treat moderate-to-severe pain and are often prescribed following surgery or injury, or for health conditions such as cancer.

The most common drugs involved in prescription opioid overdose deaths include:

Methadone

Oxycodone (such as OxyContin®)

Hydrocodone (such as Vicodin®)

Prescription opioids (like hydrocodone, oxycodone, and morphine) and illicit opioids (like heroin and illegally made fentanyl) are powerful drugs that have a risk of a potentially fatal overdose. Anyone who uses opioids can experience an overdose, but certain factors may increase risk including but not limited to:

- Combining opioids with alcohol or certain other drugs

- Taking high daily dosages of prescription opioids

- Taking more opioids than prescribed

- Taking illicit or illegal opioids, like heroin or illicitly manufactured fentanyl, that could possibly contain unknown or harmful substances

- Certain medical conditions, such as sleep apnea, or reduced kidney or liver function

- Age greater than 65 years old

Death from an opioid overdose happens when too much of the drug overwhelms the brain and interrupts the body's natural drive to breathe.

Addiction and Overdose

Anyone who takes prescription opioids can become addicted to them. In fact, as many as one in four patients receiving long-term opioid therapy in a primary care setting struggles with opioid addiction. Once addicted, it can be hard to stop.

Side Effects

In addition to the serious risks of addiction, abuse, and overdose, the use of prescription opioids can have several side effects, even when taken as directed:

- Tolerance—meaning you might need to take more of the medication for the same pain relief

- Physical dependence—meaning you have symptoms of withdrawal when the medication is stopped

- Increased sensitivity to pain

- Constipation

- Nausea, vomiting, and dry mouth

- Sleepiness and dizziness

- Confusion

- Depression

- Low levels of testosterone that can result in lower sex drive, energy, and strength

- Itching and sweating

Signs and Symptoms of an Opioid Overdose

During an overdose, breathing can be dangerously slowed or stopped, causing brain damage or death. It's important to recognize the signs and act fast. Signs include:

- Small, constricted "pinpoint pupils"
- Falling asleep or loss of consciousness
- Slow, shallow breathing
- Choking or gurgling sounds
- Limp body
- Pale, blue, or cold skin
- Foaming at the mouth

What to Do If You Think Someone Is Overdosing?

It may be hard to tell if a person is high or experiencing an overdose. If you aren't sure, it's best to treat it like an overdose— you could save a life.

1. Call 911 immediately.
2. Administer naloxone, if available. (Ask your Dr about a prescription to have on hand)
3. Try to keep the person awake and breathing.
4. Lay the person on their side to prevent choking.
5. Stay with him or her until emergency workers arrive.

Deaths

In 2004 the reported number of opioid deaths was 5,242
In 2019 the reported number of opioid deaths was 70,980

Sources:

www.cdc.gov/drugoverdose;

https://www.cdc.gov/drugoverdose/opioids/prescribed

https://www.justice.gov/archive/ndic/pubs25/25930/

https://www.aha.org/news/headline/2020-07-16-cdc-drug-over-dose-deaths-46-2019

**If you or someone you know is in crisis, PLEASE call: Substance Abuse and Mental Health Services Administration at this number-
1-800-662-4357**

ACKNOWLEDGEMENTS:

I want to thank Author Susan Pohlman for encouraging me to keep writing and for editing my first attempt at being an author. I want to thank authors Phillip Young, and Lanie Nelson for all the great advice. Also, thank you Bob Nelson for advising me and putting me in touch with people that could help with this journey. To my family and friends, thank you dear ones, you are the best. Steve Gardner and Barbara Cipolaro, thank you for being such great cheerleaders.

Made in the USA
Columbia, SC
11 March 2021